Encounter God

Manual

Jim Egli

Published by TOUCH Publications
10055 Regal Row Ste. 180
Houston, Texas, 77040, U.S.A.
(713) 896-7478 • Fax (713) 896-1874

Cover design by Don Bleyl
Text design by Rick Chandler
Editing by Scott Boren

International Standard Book Number: 1-880828-18-9

All Scripture quotations, unless otherwise indicated, are from the
Holy Bible, New International Version, Copyright © 1973, 1978, 1984
by International Bible Society.
Used by permission.

TOUCH Publications is the book-publishing division of TOUCH Outreach
Ministries, a resource and consulting ministry for churches with a vision
for cell-based local church structure.

Find us on the World Wide Web at
http://www.touchusa.org

Table of Contents

1. Understanding Spiritual Warfare 5

2a. From Darkness to the Light 13

2b. Receiving and Ministering Healing 19

3. From Bondage to Freedom 23

4. From Impure to Pure 28

5. From Broken to Whole 31

6. From Rebellion to Submission 35

7. From Cursed to Blessed 38

8. Living in Victory 42

1. Understanding Spiritual Warfare

For our struggle is not against flesh and blood, but against the rulers, against the authorities, against the powers of this dark world and against the spiritual forces of evil in the heavenly realms. (Ephesians 6:12)

➤ There is a battle going on out there! Are you fighting to win?

[handwritten: I don't aluay feel Something emotional]

NOTES

It's a War Out There!

1. Western Christians often don't realize it.

Our fight is not against flesh and blood. (Ephesians 6:12)

And there was war in heaven. . . . and . . . The great dragon was hurled down — that ancient serpent called the devil, or Satan, who leads the whole world astray. He was hurled to the earth, and his angels with him. . . . Therefore rejoice, you heavens and you who dwell in them! But woe to the earth and the sea, because the devil has gone down to you! (Revelation 12:7-12)

[handwritten notes: Its not about how you feel its how open are you to God.]

[handwritten notes: You give God your life and he has control of everything right. "NO"]

[handwritten notes: We still have our strongholds. Anger in a Christian such as a temper]

[handwritten notes: Christmas ... NEW YEAR]

5

2. The conflict of Satan and God takes place between Genesis 3:15 and Revelation 20.

3. Because of man's sin, humankind and the world are subjected to evil.

What is a Stronghold?

1. A stronghold is a heavily fortified place.

The word is used both positively and negatively in Scripture.

• God is our stronghold!

The LORD is a refuge for the oppressed, a stronghold in times of trouble. (Psalm 9:9)

The LORD is my rock, my fortress and my deliverer; my God is my rock, in whom I take refuge. He is my shield and the horn of my salvation, my stronghold. (Psalm 18:2)

• Ungodly strongholds

For though we live in the world, we do not wage war as the world does. The weapons we fight with are not the weapons of the world. On the contrary, they have divine power to demolish strongholds. (2 Corinthians 10:3-4)

The Israelites took the land but parts of it were out of their control.

In the same way, though we have given our life to Christ, some areas may be "out of control."

Examples: anger, lust, fear, resentment.

2. A stronghold is ground Satan gains in our lives through entry points.

> *"In your anger do not sin": Do not let the sun go down while you are still angry, and do not give the devil a foothold.*
> (Ephesians 4:25-26)

> *See to it that no one misses the grace of God and that no bitter root grows up to cause trouble and defile many.* (Hebrews 12:15)

3. Strongholds can come from:

- Sin (Particularly habitual sin)
- Unforgiveness
- Occult Involvement
- Generational Bondage
- Traumatic Life Experiences

4. What is a stronghold? A hold that is strong!

It is usually futile to try to remove spiritual oppression without dealing with the root.

Handwritten note: Adultry to The Lord

Jesus already died to free us from ALL of these bondages! No further price must be paid!

We have all Authority in Christ!

The authority of a police officer does not come from his or her experience, rank or training.

Every Christian has the full authority of Christ over evil forces.

We are already in position above and over forces of evil.

In his book *Resolving Spiritual Conflicts & Cross-Cultural Ministry*, Dr. Timothy Warner explains three worldviews:

1. In "The Dominant Worldview," God is removed from the world. People try to manipulate spiritual forces through mediums or holy men.

The "Dominant" Worldview

God
God is removed from the world. People try to manipulate spiritual forces through mediums or holy men.

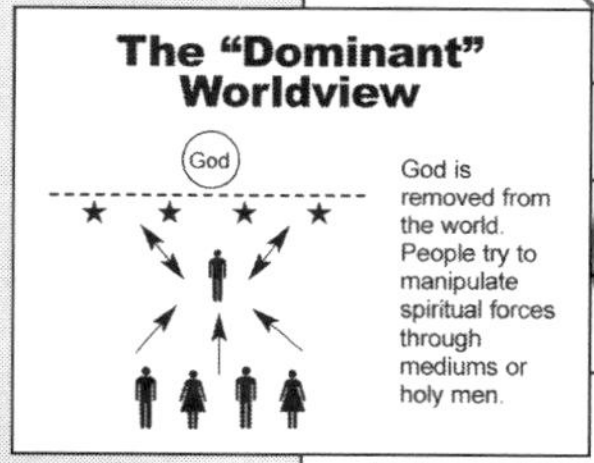

2. In "The Scientific Worldview," God is removed from the world. The only reality is the material world. People are on their own.

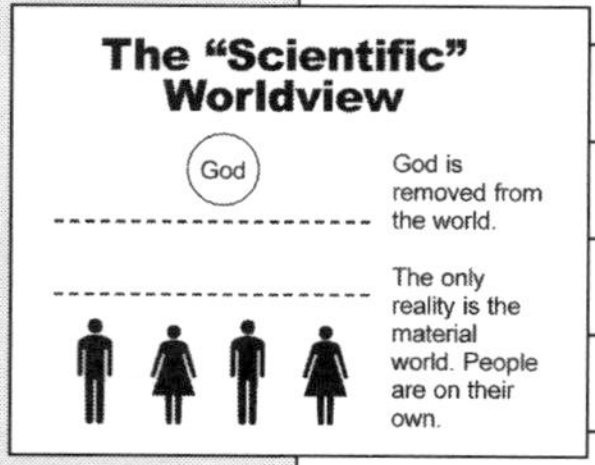

The "Scientific" Worldview

God
God is removed from the world.

The only reality is the material world. People are on their own.

Handwritten notes in margin:
Policemen Has Authority from the first time he puts on the uniform. It you get stopped do you ask
How long have you been a police officer?
OR What is your Rank?
Because he has authority. NOT power Like picking up a CAR

3. However, in "The Biblical World-view," God is active and interested in the world. There are both good and evil spiritual beings (angels).

The "Biblical" Worldview

God is active & interested in the world.

There are both good and evil spiritual beings (angels).

God works through angels and by His Spirit. The Spirit guides believers and convicts unbelievers.

The "Biblical" Worldview

God works through angels and by His Spirit.

The Spirit guides Believers & Convicts Unbelievers.

Fallen angels have two primary means to influence people: temptation and deception.

The "Biblical" Worldview

Fallen angels have two primary means to influence people. . .

We are seated with Christ: *"And God raised us up with Christ and seated us with him in the heavenly realms in Christ Jesus . . ."* (Ephesians 2:6)

The Authority of Christ

Christ has "all authority in heaven and earth."

Why is it so hard to take the power that God has given us. We take it in everything else.

When we look at life
through a Christian
Worldview, we see that
seated with Christ we
approach spiritual warfare
from a position ABOVE
evil forces!

Our Authority in Christ

We approach spiritual warfare from a position ABOVE evil forces!

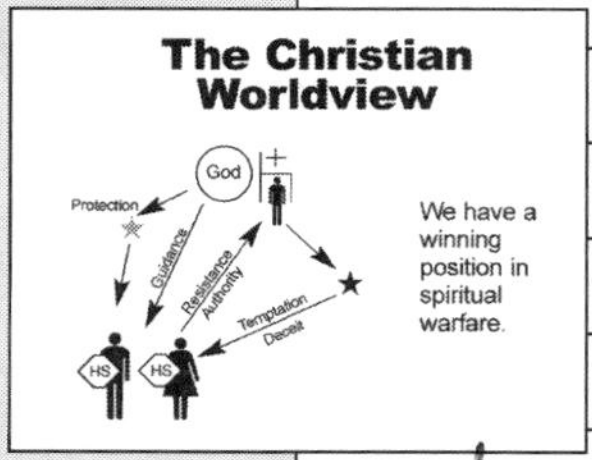

The Christian Worldview

We have a winning position in spiritual warfare.

[handwritten note: define sin]

[handwritten note: Sin is putting ourselves on the throne of our lives.]

[handwritten note: Anything in violation of God word.]

Understanding Sin and Spiritual Warfare

1. The heart is not only wicked above
   all things; it is *deceitfully* wicked!
   (Jeremiah 17:9)

   Deception is such a powerful tool
   because the deceived person does
   not know it!

2. Our nuclear arsenal

- Divine power to tear down
  arguments and pretensions and to
  take captive every thought.
- God's Word has explosive power to
  tear down strongholds.

3. Sin is . . .

- Putting ourselves on the throne of
  our lives.

10

- Anything in violation of God's Word. (see Genesis 3:1-8)

4. We don't need to know about evil.

   . . . but I want you to be wise about what is good, and innocent about what is evil. (Romans 16:19)

[handwritten note: I don't even know what you are talking about. Like a newborn Baby]

5. Be aware of the idols of Entertainment, Materialism, Comfort, and Personal Freedom that are worshiped in our culture.

The Reality

1. Jesus wants the best for us, Satan wants the worst:

   "The thief comes only to steal and kill and destroy; I have come that they may have life, and have it to the full. I am the good shepherd. The good shepherd lays down his life for the sheep." (John 10:10-11)

[handwritten note: Satan is here to destroy. Jesus came to give us life.]

2. God's heart

   May God himself, the God of peace, sanctify you through and through.

   May your whole spirit, soul and body be kept blameless at the coming of our Lord Jesus Christ. The one who calls you is faithful and he will do it.
   (1 Thessalonians 5:23-24)

What Do You Want?

Do you want Christ's total freedom?

Write a short prayer from your heart to Christ on the front page of your Spiritual Freedom Inventory.

2a. From Darkness to the Light

But you are a chosen people, a royal priesthood, a holy nation,
a people belonging to God, that you may declare the praises of him
who called you out of darkness into his
wonderful light. (1 Peter 2:9)

➤ Are you walking in the light?

The Thief

Satan is out to rob you of life. He does this through temptation and deception:

- In temptation he makes the destructive look inviting.
- He seeks to deceive us
  - About ourselves
  - About God
  - About right/wrong/ judgement

Our Powerful Arsenal

The weapons we fight with are not the weapons of the world. On the contrary, they have divine power to demolish strongholds. We demolish arguments and every pretension that sets itself up against the knowledge of God, and we take

captive every thought to make it obedient to Christ.
(2 Corinthians 10:4-5)

Our weapons:

- The shed blood of Christ — His victory won upon Calvary.
- The truth of the Word of God — to overcome temptation and to shatter the lies of the evil one.
- The gifts of the Spirit — words of knowledge, discerning of spirits, faith, healing, miracles.
(1 Corinthians 12:8ff)

The Power of Confession

- To confess *(homologeo)* in the New Testament means, "to agree or concede."
- To confess Jesus as Lord (Romans 10:9-10) means to "concede" or to yield to His Lordship.
- To confess our sins means to "agree" or admit that we did it.

1. Confession brings forgiveness.

If we confess our sins, he is faithful and just and will forgive us our sins and purify us from all unrighteousness. (1 John 1:9)

2. Confession releases healing.

Therefore confess your sins to each other and pray for each other so that you may be healed.
(James 5:16)

Handwritten notes: Deal with the Root. Can't just pray and pray & pray. CONFESSION Forgiveness means Going to God. You don't have to go to tell someone else to be forgiven. You confess to others in order to be Healed

14

- "Healed" *(iaomai)*: cured, healed, made whole.
- The nature of sin is to hide what we are doing. Confession disables sin by bringing it into the light.
- Confession brings support, prayer, release and pardon.

If you forgive anyone his sins, they are forgiven . . .
(John 20:23)

We Can Experience Jesus' Freedom

- From Darkness to Light: Freedom from False Religions and the Occult
- From Bondage to Freedom: Release from Habitual Sins and Addictions
- From Impure to Pure: Sexual Freedom
- From Broken to Whole: Release from Resentment and Anger
- From Rebellion to Submission
- From Cursed to Blessed

From Darkness to the Light

Freedom from false religion and occult involvement

1. Satan's goal is to rob you and neutralize you through . . .

- Religious deception
- Spiritual bondage
- Diluted fidelity to the Lord Jesus Christ

Handwritten notes:
You Give +
Take away

Means

He gives us Freedom
& Peace Forgiveness
Peace etc . . .

He takes away
anger, & guilt,
shame etc . . .

2. Every spiritual power that is not in Jesus' name is evil.

• People may experience power or healing, but there is a corresponding bondage!
• Satan appears as an "angel of light." (2 Corinthians 11:14)

3. God wants the best for you!

• He does not want you robbed by Satan.
• God is also very jealous for your devotion.
• So he commands total avoidance of ALL other spiritual influences.

You shall have no other gods before me. You shall not make for yourself an idol in the form of anything in heaven above or on the earth beneath or in the waters below. You shall not bow down to them or worship them; for I, the LORD your God, am a jealous God, punishing the children for the sin of the fathers to the third and fourth generation of those who hate me, but showing love to a thousand generations of those who love me and keep my commandments. (Exodus 20:3-6)

You shall have no foreign god among you; you shall not bow down to an alien god. (Psalm 81:9)

Let no one be found among you who . . . practices divination or sorcery, interprets omens, engages in witchcraft, or casts spells, or who is a medium or spiritist or who consults the dead. Anyone who does these things is detestable to the LORD. (Deuteronomy 18:10-12)

4. Satan wants to divide your devotion and trust.

   "Even while these people were worshipping the LORD, they were serving their idols." (2 Kings 17:41)

   a. God considers any divided allegiance as spiritual adultery.

      • How much of their spouse's attention does a husband or wife want given to someone else?
      • Dabbling is serious to God & damaging to us.

   b. The current fascination with angels is also an old attempt of Satan to divert attention from Jesus. (Colossians 2:18-19)

5. Jesus offers total freedom from spiritual bondage.

   When you were dead in your sins . . . God made you alive with Christ . . . And having disarmed the powers and authorities, he made a public spectacle of them, triumphing over them by the cross. (Colossians 2:13-15)

[Handwritten notes:] Worshiping ? God and still serving Idols

[Handwritten notes:] well they can flirt a little or kiss someone a little God wants full attention and all of our love. Adultry is what God views of our giving any attention to something else.

17

Spiritual Bondage

- We should confess all involvement in false religions and philosophies.
- We should confess generational involvement of our ancestors.
- Even "small" matters, or things done "for fun," are dilutions of trust in Christ. (horoscope, 8 Balls, etc.)

Any supposed "positive" benefit is part of the deception.

Mark Areas of Involvement

On your Spiritual Freedom Inventory:

- Place a check in the left box in areas you experienced in the PAST.
- Place a check in the right box in areas you are dealing with in the PRESENT.
- Circle areas that your FAMILY has or is experiencing.
- Do just the "Darkness to Light" area!

You will have an opportunity to destroy your Spiritual Freedom Inventory before the close of the retreat.

Possible Oppressive Spirits Associated with False Religion and The Occult

- Curiosity
- Witchcraft
- False Religion
- Deception
- Control
- Rationalization

2b. Receiving and Ministering Healing

. . . confess your sins to each other and pray for each other
so that you may be healed.
(James 5:16a)

➤ Do you want to be healed?

How Do We Receive Healing?

God gives us two commands in James 5:16:

• Confess your sin to one another.
• Pray for one another.

The guide for receiving healing is located on the back cover of this manual.

A Healing Pattern

Your part in your healing:

• Submit to God
• Confess

Other's part — prayer
(a simple acrostic):

- **A**ssure forgiveness
- **B**reak bondage
- **C**ast away oppression
- **D**estroy images
- **E**xtend God's healing

Your Part-Submit

*Submit yourselves, then, to God.
Resist the devil, and he will flee
from you. Come near to God and
he will come near to you.*
(James 4:7-8)

- We will sometimes say a submission
  prayer as a group.
- If you sense blockage at any time,
  pray and submit yourself in that
  area to the Lord.
- This in itself will often bring
  immediate spiritual freedom.

Your Part – Confess

1. Confession simply means admitting
   your sin in a straightforward
   prayer.

- You do not need to go into details.
- You do not need to plead with God.
- A recommended prayer is given on
  the back of this manual.

2. Let the Holy Spirit bring things to
   mind.

3. Confess areas for healing you may have prayed about previously so that they can be ministered to in a thorough way.

Six Steps to Minister Healing:

1. A simple prayer of confession:

Heavenly Father, I confess
_____ as my sin. I repent of it and I ask you to forgive me.

Ministry from/to others

2. **As**sure forgiveness based on God's Word. (A possible statement is clearly printed for you on the back cover.)

3. **B**reak bondages to any:

• People
• Places
• Things
• Feelings

4. **Cast** away.

• Sense God's timing. (You may ask the person at times if they sense anything.)
• Refer to the possible bondage areas on the Spiritual Freedom Inventory.
• Do not be overly concerned with this area.

5. **Destroy** images.

6. **Extend** God's healing love to restore.

Important Instructions

1. Do ONE person at a time.

- That person should confess his or her sin.
- THEN the other(s) should minister to him or her following the healing pattern.
- Do NOT move to the second person until you are done with the first person. (If you jump back and forth, aspects of ministry get dropped.)

2. What if someone does not want ministry?

- If someone does not want to share or to bring an area to God, accept that.
- Offer everyone all the ministry they desire but never force ministry.

3. From Bondage to Freedom

... live by the spirit, and you will not gratify the desires of the sinful nature.
(Galatians 5:16)

➤ Are you seeking to please yourself or the Spirit?

In This Session We'll Deal With. . .

• Destructive Attitudes
• Destructive Habits
• Idolatry
• Addictions and Dependency

Destructive Attitudes

The acts of the sinful nature are obvious: sexual immorality, impurity and debauchery; idolatry and witchcraft; hatred, discord, jealousy, fits of rage, selfish ambition, dissensions, factions and envy; drunkenness, orgies, and the like.
(Galatians 5:19-21)

Are any of these in your life?

- Jealousy
- Self-pity
- People-pleasing
  (being controlled by a desire to
  please others)
- Envy
- Hatred
- Unforgiveness and Grudges
- Vengeance
- Anger
- Argumentativeness
- Covetousness (wanting what
  belongs to others)
- Greed

*You cannot serve both God and
Money.* (Matthew 6:24)

- Perfectionism
- Unbelief

Destructive Habits and Actions

- Gossip
- Hurtful Speech (Ephesians 4:29)
- Dirty Language
- Cursing
- Stealing
- Lying
- Breaking Promises
- Murder
- Death Wish
  (for someone or self)

Idolatry

Blind or excessive devotion to something. (American Heritage Dictionary)

Idolatry is putting something in place of God — looking to it for fulfillment and meaning rather than God.

- You can idolize a person, past time or thing.
- On your Freedom Inventory, write down anything you have idolized.

Addiction or Dependency on:

- Gluttony
- Nicotine
- Mind-Altering Drugs
- Alcohol
- Gambling
- Credit Cards
- Excessive Computer Use
- Television
- Other(s)?

If you have a serious addiction, you may need to do other things in addition to praying over the area today:

- Seek ongoing accountability.
- Get rid of anything that contributes to the bondage. (Trash the trash!)
- Are you willing to do this?
- Hate the sin and avoid tempting situations.
- Find a support group.

Healing Pattern Review

Your part in your healing:

• Submit to God
• Confess

Other's part — prayer

• **A**ssure forgiveness
• **B**reak bondage
• **C**ast away oppression
• **D**estroy images
• **E**xtend God's healing

Important Instructions

• Resist the temptation to counsel.
• Follow the sequence of the pattern.
• Listen to the Holy Spirit's voice and timing.

Joint Prayer of Submission

Heavenly Father, You have called me to clothe myself with Christ and "not to gratify the desires of the sinful nature."

God, I now choose to turn from all destructive habits, actions and attitudes and to rely only on you. I choose to walk in obedience to your Word and your Spirit.

Through the power of Jesus' shed blood I claim your total freedom. Amen.

Possible areas of oppression related to habitual sins, idolatry, and addictions.

- Curiosity
- False Religion
- Deception

- Idolatry
- Control
- Fear

4. From Impure to Pure

May God himself, the God of peace, sanctify you through and through. May your whole spirit, soul and body be kept blameless at the coming of our Lord Jesus Christ.
(1 Thessalonians 5:23)

➤ In Christ we can be pure spiritually, emotionally, and physically!

God's Good Gift

1. Our sexuality is a beautiful gift from God to be kept pure and holy.

- Because our sexuality is a powerful part of how God has made us, it often becomes misdirected.
- Our sexuality is like a beautiful river, lovely as it flows within its banks, but it becomes a flood of destruction if it flows outside its bounds.

2. God calls us to purity of body, heart and mind.

Be holy, because I am the LORD your God. (Leviticus 20:7)

I will set before my eyes no vile thing. (Psalm 101:3)

28

Finally, brothers, whatever is true, whatever is noble, whatever is right, whatever is pure, whatever is lovely, whatever is admirable — if anything is excellent or praiseworthy — think about such things. . . .and the God of PEACE will be with you.
(Philippians 4:8, 9b)

There is a peace in purity!

3. Satan's lie

Satan tells us that we must be in the "know."

We have often believed Satan's lie, allowing his destruction into our minds.

However, God calls us to innocence.

Brothers, stop thinking like children. In regard to evil be infants, but in your thinking be adults.
(1 Corinthians 14:20)

. . . I want you to be wise about what is good, and innocent about what is evil.
(Romans 16:19)

But among you there must not be even a hint of sexual immorality, or of any kind of impurity, or of greed, because these are improper for God's holy people.
(Ephesians 5:3)

Soul Ties

1. Sexual union creates a oneness.
   (1 Corinthians 6:16)

- This is intended for good in the context of marriage.
- Outside of marriage it creates bondage and an entry for demonic influence.

2. Cutting soul ties (bondage to people and things) is important in this section.

Jesus offers us total freedom as we renounce and cut all ties.

3. God offers us total purity.

May God himself, the God of peace, sanctify you through and through. May your whole spirit, soul and body be kept blameless at the coming of our Lord Jesus Christ.
(1 Thessalonians 5:23)

Possible areas of oppression related to Sexual Impurity.

- Curiosity
- Lust
- Self-gratification
- Low self-esteem

- Sensuality
- Rationalization
- Perversion
- False guilt (if abused)

5. From Broken to Whole

But he was pierced for our transgressions, he was crushed for our iniquities; the punishment that brought us peace was upon him, and by his wounds we are healed. (Isaiah 53:5)

➤ Jesus died for all the wrong we have done and all the wrongs done to us.

Life in a Fallen World

1. Like Joseph in the Old Testament, we live in a fallen, unjust world.

- Pain
- Abandonment
- Abuse
- Ridicule and prejudice
- Hurt & hurting others — Family, work, friends, spouse

2. Our hurt and pain create

- Loneliness
- Rejection
- Resentment
- Fear
- Anger

3. Christ's victory offers us:

• Release from resentment
• Wholeness in place of brokenness
• "Beauty for Ashes"
• "Joy for Mourning"
• "Praise instead of Despair"
  (Isaiah 61:3)

Our Part: Forgive!

1. Forgive . . .

To forgive means to "release"

• It is an act of the will
• To take hurt upon oneself

Forgiving and trusting are not the same.

• Trust must often be rebuilt, but we can always forgive.

We forgive for our own sake.

God stands ready to help us forgive.

2. Unforgiveness is not an option!

And when you stand praying, if you hold anything against anyone, forgive him, so that your Father in heaven may forgive you your sins. (Jesus, Mark 11:25)

Forgive us our sins, for we also forgive everyone who sins against us. (Luke 11:4)

Be kind and compassionate to one another, forgiving each other, just as in Christ God forgave you.
(Ephesians 4:32)

Forgiveness Exercise

On your Spiritual Freedom Inventory:

• Write the NAME of the persons you need to forgive in the left column.
• Enter the OFFENSES against you in the middle column.
• Write the FEELINGS you experienced in the right column.

With Your Ministry Partner

• If it is helpful, talk with your partner about what you wrote down before you pray.

Prayer of Forgiveness

Heavenly Father, I choose to forgive
name of the person
for *the offense(s).*
This made me feel
emotion experienced.

- Before or after this, confess any sin you committed in this relationship.
- Proceed through the healing steps.
- You do not have time to forgive everyone for everything now. As God brings more to mind in the days ahead, take time to forgive.

Possible areas of oppression related to Hurt and Unforgiveness.

- Resentment
- Anger
- Revenge
- Rejection
- Failure
- Loneliness
- Low Self-Esteem or Inferiority

- Indecision
- Fear
- Doubt
- Rebellion
- Lust
- Perversion

6. From Rebellion to Submission

Many times he delivered them, but they were bent on rebellion and they wasted away in their sin.
(Psalm 106:43)

➤ Are you willing to give up your rights?

Rebellion

"An act or a show of defiance toward an authority or established convention." (American Heritage Dictionary)

1. Rebellion is at the root of all sin. "I will do things my way!"

• We live in a rebellious time, in a rebellious culture and nation.
• Rebellion opens us to Satanic attack and deception.

2. We rebel against . . .

• God
• Parents
• Teachers
• Church
• Government (Taxes, Laws)
• Boss
• Husband
• Others?

3. God calls us to submit to God-given authorities.

Submit yourselves for the Lord's sake to every authority instituted among men: whether to the king, as the supreme authority, or to governors, who are sent by him . . .
(1 Peter 2:13)

Submit to one another out of reverence for Christ.
(Ephesians 5:21)

The only time we are called to rebel is when submission to an authority would involve disobedience to God.

4. Unforgiveness is often a source of rebellion and rejection.

• If you have trouble submitting, you may need to stop and forgive.

We are hurt and feel rejected, and in response we rebel.

Rebellion takes many forms:

Complaining

Do everything without complaining or arguing, so that you may become blameless and pure, children of God without fault in a crooked and depraved generation.
(Philippians 2:14-15)

*You are not grumbling against us,
but against the LORD.*
(Moses said in Exodus 16:8)

- Judging others
- Self-righteousness
- Negative attitude
- Pride or arrogance
- Racism (It is actually corporate or national arrogance)
- Vandalism
- Violence

Prayer of Submission to God

*Heavenly Father, you have declared that "rebellion is like the sin of
divination, and arrogance like the evil of idolatry." I have rebelled
against you in my attitudes and actions. I now choose to submit to
you and the authorities you have placed in my life. I turn from
rebellion, pride and complaining. I ask you to give me a thankful,
submissive heart.*
In the name of Jesus my Master. Amen

*For rebellion is like the sin of
divination, and arrogance like the
evil of idolatry. Because you have
rejected the word of the LORD, he
has rejected you as king.*
(1 Samuel 15:23)

Possible Oppressive Spirits Related to Rebellion and Arrogance.

- Self-pity
- Self-will
- Pride
- Competitive Spirit
- Rejection

- Rebellion
- Revenge or Vengeful Spirit
- Control
- Witchcraft
- Unforgiveness (Possible ring-leader

7. From Cursed to Blessed

Christ redeemed us from the curse of the law by becoming a curse for us, for it is written: "Cursed is everyone who is hung on a tree." He redeemed us in order that the blessing given to Abraham might come to the Gentiles through Christ Jesus, so that by faith we might receive the promise of the Spirit. (Galatians 3:13-14)

➤ Christ has broken the power of curses and generational bondage!

NOTES

The Power of Blessing

1. Our hearts long for blessing.

The story of Isaac, Jacob and Esau in Genesis 27 reveals the power of blessing and the tragedy of blessing withheld.

- We all yearn for love, affirmation and unconditional acceptance.
- There is an emptiness when we fail to receive it.
- There is power in the tongue to bless and to curse. (Proverbs 18:21)
- Today God's blessing is offered to all of us through Christ. (Galatians 3:14)

2. What is a life-giving blessing?

The five elements in this definition are from Chapter 2 of the excellent book *The Blessing* by Gary Smalley and John Trent. Blessing involves:

- Meaningful touch
- A spoken word
- Attaching high value to the one being blessed
- Picturing a special future
- An active commitment to fulfill the blessings

What is a Curse?

- Condemning or demeaning words from others or ourselves
- Withheld love, touch or commitment
- Spiritual bondage created by sin (Exodus 20:5)
- Declared bondage and consequences from vows

From Cursed to Blessed

1. The Bible calls us to reverse the flow of curses by blessing those who curse us.

- Luke 6:27-28
- Romans 12:14, 21
- 1 Peter 3:9

2. On the cross Jesus took upon Himself every curse that we or others have brought on us.

- Galatians 3:13-14
- Isaiah 53:3-6
- 2 Corinthians 5:21

To Receive Your Own Freedom:

1. Complete the "Cursed to Blessed" section of your inventory and discuss it with your ministry partner.

2. Confess any sin of yourself or your ancestors. (People in Scripture often confessed the sins of their ancestors to break bondage and release blessing. See, for example, Jeremiah 14:20; Daniel 9:8: and Nehemiah 1:6.) Be sure to confess as sin any ungodly vows that you (or ancestors) have made.

3. Specifically forgive any people who hurt you, cursed you or let you down in the areas you are praying through.

4. Renounce any curse that has been brought against you. You can pray the prayer below or something similar.

Prayer to Release Curses

Heavenly Father, I believe that on the cross Jesus took every curse that could ever be spoken or brought against me and my family. So I ask you now to release me from every curse over my life. I also claim total release of my family from all of these curses. In the name of Jesus, I specifically break the curses of _____. By faith, I receive total release and I thank you for it.

To Minister to Someone Else:

After the person has completed the above steps, in the name of Jesus:

A. Assure them of their forgiveness if they sinned.

B. Break all bondages to the relevant people, organizations and experiences.

C. Cast away any spiritual oppression in Jesus' name.

D. Destroy any words or images.

E. Extend God's healing power in prayer. Minister any words, truth or Scriptures that come to your mind.

8. Living in Victory

It is for freedom that Christ has set us free. Stand firm, then, and do not let yourselves be burdened again by a yoke of slavery.
(Galatians 5:1)

➤ God's Word offers powerful principles for daily victory and freedom!

Jesus said:

To a healed paralytic:

"See, you are well again. Stop sinning or something worse may happen to you." (John 5:14)

To the woman caught in adultery:

"Then neither do I condemn you. Go now and leave your life of sin."
(John 8:11)

Living in Victory

- Getting set free is easy.
- Staying set free is harder!
- But God's Word gives us powerful principles to enable us to walk in freedom.

You adulterous people, don't you know that friendship with the world is hatred towards God? Anyone who chooses to be a friend of the world becomes an enemy of God. . . . Submit yourselves, then, to God. Resist the devil, and he will flee from you. Come near to God and he will come near to you. Wash your hands, you sinners, and purify your hearts, you double-minded. (James 4:4, 7-8)

First, Realize You Have an Enemy who Hates You!

1. Satan wants to steal your joy and ruin your life, your relationships and your loved ones!

   "The thief comes only to steal and kill and destroy; I have come that they may have life, and have it to the full." (John 10:10)

2. Choose to hate evil.

- *To fear the LORD is to <u>hate evil</u>.* (Proverbs 8:13)
- *<u>Hate</u> evil, love good.* (Amos 5:15)
- *<u>Hate</u> what is evil; cling to what is good.* (Romans 12:9)
- Develop a hatred toward evil (greed, lust, resentment, etc.) because Satan uses them to destroy you and those you love!

Hate evil
is to fear the Lord.
love

Billy Ray

43

You have two choices!

> *"You adulterous people, don't you know that friendship with the world is hatred towards God? Anyone who chooses to be a friend of the world becomes an enemy of God."*
> (James 4:4)

> *"Do not love the world or anything in the world. If anyone loves the world, the love of the Father is not in him."* (1 John 2:15)

- Choose! *"As for me and my house, we will serve the Lord."* (Joshua 24:15)

What do *YOU* need to hate?

Where are you most easily tempted or sidetracked?

What do you need to hate in order to avoid the trap of these temptations?

Second, Submit to God!

1. Surrender to Christ

- Have you determined that you want Christ to rule every area of your life (finances, family, career, thoughts and actions)? If not, do that today!

- Lord, I choose obedience to you in every area and every decision in my life.

2. Enjoy God daily

- Find a quiet time and place.
- Take a consistent, generous amount of time.
- Do whatever you enjoy (reading the Bible, prayer, journaling, worshiping).
- Include time to just listen to Him.

3. If you struggle . . .

- Pray about it.
- Identify why you do not take the time.
  - What are the obstacles?
  - Identify the strongholds and bring them to God.
- Talk to those close to you to get their cooperation in helping you take time with God.

What do *YOU* need to do?

What do you need to do right now to move forward in your relationship with Christ?

What obstacles stand in the way?

Third, Resist the Devil!

1. Receive God's protection and blessing through prayer.

• Pray for God's peace and truth to fill your home. (Luke 10:5, John 16:13)

• Pray for God's deliverance from temptation. (Matthew 6:11; Luke 22:40)

2. Put on God's armor each day. (Ephesians 6:14-18)

• Helmet of Salvation
• Breastplate of Righteousness
• Belt of Truth
• Gospel of Peace on Your Feet
• Shield of Faith and Sword of the Spirit

3. Destroy everything ungodly that is in your possession.

• If there are things in your home that belong to others which you cannot destroy, seal them with the blood of Christ to keep evil forces from operating through them.

4. Avoid temptation

God calls us to be wise more often than He calls us to be strong.

• Jesus tells us to pray for deliverance from temptation itself. (Matthew 6:11; Luke 22:40)

- The assumption seems to be that we cave in easily!

Avoid tempting situations and relationships.

Anticipate and cut off the Enemy's strategies!

Submit yourselves, then, to God. Resist the devil, and he will flee from you. (James 4:7)

How can *YOU* Avoid Temptation?

What do you need to get rid of or destroy?

What are some specific situations or relationships that you should avoid, or actions you should take to eliminate or minimize temptations?

About Jim Egli . . .

Jim Egli and his wife Vicki serve as Small Group Pastors at the Champaign (IL) Vineyard overseeing a growing system of over 50 cell groups and target groups. He serves as a Trainer and Curriculum Consultant with TOUCH spearheading the Encounter God initiative. Jim is also the Director of Research for Missions International. He is completing a Ph.D. in Communication at Regent University. He and his wife Vicki have three young adult sons and a nine-year-old daughter.